MEMORY

MOVEMENT

MEMORY

OBJECTS

MEMORY

MOVEMENT

MEMORY

OBJECTS

ALICE ANDERSON

First published in 2015 by Wellcome Collection,
part of The Wellcome Trust,
215 Euston Road, London NW1 2BE

wellcomecollection.org

A CIP catalogue record for this book is available from
the British Library.

ISBN 978-0-9570285-4-8

Commissioning Editor: Kirty Topiwala
Designer: Liam Relph
Ancillary text: Kate Forde
Assistant Editor: Tom Freeman
Production Co-ordinator: Petra Essing
Photography: Matt Holyoak
Additional photography: Joe Lang, Jose Segui,
Jose Ruiz, Marcela Iriarte, Alice Anderson,
Rupert Barth von Wehrenalp
Lighting Design: Rupert Barth von Wehrenalp
Photography post-production: Jon Griffiths

Printed and bound in China by C&C Offset Printing

Any omissions and errors of attribution are unintentional
and will, if notified in writing to the editor, care of
Wellcome Trust, be corrected in future printings.

All the artworks shown here were exhibited
at the Wellcome Collection exhibition
Alice Anderson: Memory Movement Memory Objects,
curated by Kate Forde and are reproduced by the
artist's kind permission.

wellcomecollection.org/aliceanderson

CONTENTS

—

Geometrical Shapes, 2014.

THE ART OF MEMORY

–

BY KATE FORDE

Alice Anderson's new work asks you to take a journey into memory. Walking through a series of rooms you will encounter shapes that seem at once familiar and strange – a car, a record-player, sketch books, a bicycle, even a staircase have been transformed into glowing trophies – lending the experience a hallucinatory quality. Each item has been tightly bound with copper wire, which preserves its outline but removes its function. Divested of purpose these mute objects appear suspended in time, compelling you to rediscover what you thought you already knew intimately. Some may remind you of your own belongings, a few will prompt reminiscences about things you loved then discarded, some will remain abstract and enigmatic. A number of sculptures are presented 'naked' – as work in progress – so you may, if you wish, bring about their transformation by helping to 'mummify' them in the gallery. As you move through each space the works become increasingly mysterious and distorted as they respond to the pressure of the metal thread and morph into even more curious forms. This is no invitation to nostalgic reverie but a request to be fully awake and conscious of your own ability to weave memories in the here and now.

DISEMBODIED
MEMORY

We live in a world in which the art of memory seems almost obsolete, having been first consigned to the printed page and now outsourced to communications technology, through which images and information are endlessly uploaded and reproduced. These contemporary methods of digital record-keeping led Anderson to think about the impact they might have upon our perception of ourselves and the world, ultimately triggering a new direction in her practice. In response to the idea that memories were becoming disembodied and living online, her work took a decisively sculptural turn.

In the studio one morning in 2011, Anderson began to wind copper wire around her video camera, a charged act for an artist who had started out as a film maker. Finding the work surprisingly satisfying, she spent the whole day on it without noticing; next morning, when she returned, the bound object seemed to her to be 'protected' like a time capsule or a mummified treasure from a Pharaoh's tomb. Anderson quickly resolved to apply this technique to the other objects and furniture in her studio, soon moving on to its architectural elements including the doors, steps and window frames. Having irrevocably changed the status of these things, she is committed to a future living without them, and has determined never to replace what is 'done'. The reincarnation first realised in her series 'Weaving in the Studio' (2011) was in part an attempt to preserve items from Anderson's past life, and, as she puts it, to prevent them from disappearing. But these works also demonstrate that even those objects that speak to us because of their enduring familiarity are fundamentally altered by our experience of time.

With this latest work Anderson is exploring one of science's most startling discoveries about the process of remembering. Rather than fixing our histories, it appears the brain is malleable, and functions by continually reimagining the past, connecting together what Israel Rosenfield in his essay refers to as a "flow of perceptions".

Opposite, above:
Mummified objects
in Anderson's studio.
Opposite, below:
Anderson with
Skeletons, Apple Mac
Plugs in progress, 2013.

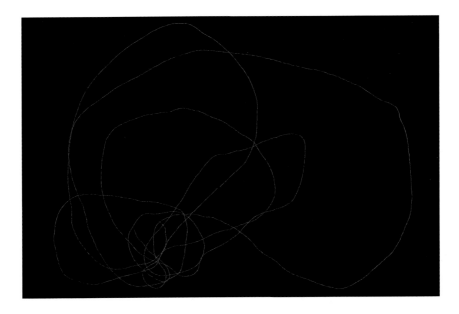

Above and right:
Nocturnal Drawing, 2011.
Part of a series of night
performance pieces in which
Anderson moves around black
paper in a ritual dance, while
holding copper thread in her
hands and feet.

While this understanding represents a radical departure from the psychological and philosophical approaches which dominated the study of the brain during the 20th century, its emphasis on the unstable and profoundly creative nature of recollection finds echoes in the way our ancestors practised the art of memory.

COLLECTIVE REMEMBRANCE

In the oral culture of Ancient Greece the survival of legends was entrusted to the Muses, the daughters of Mnemosyne, goddess of memory. It was their task to ensure that valiant heroes and fearsome gods did not drift into silent obscurity, a feat they achieved by bestowing upon mortals the gifts of poetry and song. In pre-literate society, therefore, the passing on of history is an undeniably imaginative act, the poem is recited, sung and reinterpreted by an audience already familiar with its theme. In this fleeting exchange collective identity is reinforced, and meaning is conveyed not merely through words but through the performing body. These ideas about the active nature of recollection, the ability of physical communication to convey meaning, and the reciprocal relationship between the artist and her audience all find expression in Anderson's practice. They also remind us that memory, as Oliver Sacks has written, "is dialogic and arises not only from direct experience but from the intercourse of many minds".

James Putnam has eloquently described the way in which Anderson "performs" her work, using her hands, feet and entire body to manipulate red fibre, copper wire and thread, turning rhythmical movements into drawing, installation and sculpture. This emphasis on the body as medium is liberating for the way it enables an emotional and intuitive as well as intellectual reading of the work. It evokes Maurice Merleau-Ponty's insight that vision and the body are tangled up in one another and that we cannot hope to observe existence or to understand art from afar.

Anderson's practice may also remind us of another artist, Eva Hesse, whose sculpture has bodily connotations and who was similarly concerned with the literalness of materials and the importance of process. Like Hesse, Anderson draws upon the vocabulary and aesthetic of minimalism while challenging its rigid commitment to objectivity and attempt to purge metaphor and self-expression from form. Anderson's 'Ropes' is a tribute to Hesse's 'Untitled (Rope Piece)', made in 1970 while she was dying and finished with the help of her friends. While Hesse's snarled web of latex-coated string has a visceral quality, Anderson's 'Ropes' are supple, lustrous coils of energy. Both sculptures can be reorganised and hung in any number of different ways, both are acknowledgements that the artist's intention is only one of the factors governing the work's final shape, and that art making occurs within a social situation.

THE
STUDIO

The association between Hesse and Anderson is a corrective to the myth of the artist as a 'divinely inspired' prodigy and the misconception that artworks function as direct translations of personal experience. Instead the works testify to the creative act as an ongoing process of learning and experimentation that is always in dialogue with others. When Anderson first began working on the larger elements in her studio she invited a group of people along to help, and she has explained how this collective action produced patterns of movement and even music as the bobbins of thread rattled in their ceramic jars. Inspired by the energy generated by this event and people's enthusiasm to join in, Anderson set up the Travelling Studio – an itinerant space in which participants perform within the defined convention but formulate their own gestures and methods of mummifying and their own understanding of what it is they are doing. Evoking the spirit of Andy Warhol's Factory (the name he gave to his New York studio between 1962 and 1968), Anderson's space

Opposite:
Vinyls in progress, 2013.

is the latest in a series of experiments into collaborative artistic practice. Refuting the idea of the individual artist working in isolation, Anderson's work expresses her own belief in art as a powerfully charged communal ritual.

In 1957, Marcel Duchamp gave a lecture in which he explained that "the work of art is not performed by the artist alone" and that the spectator's point of view affects the all-important "transubstantiation" of inert matter into art. What is blandly referred to now as audience participation was for Duchamp a mystical process, a way of overcoming the habit of seeing artworks as self-sufficient entities. This was achieved by acknowledging that the art object's meaning was defined by contingent factors such as the gallery context and the associations people would inevitably bring to bear. Anderson's latest works enable a similar conversion to take place: poised between abstraction and representation they rely on our readiness to interpret them liberally, to awaken our own memories and give instinct free rein. In Anderson's case we are invited not only to interact with the work but to become involved in the process of making it; the democratic spirit of the enterprise is pushed to its conclusion and the boundary between artist and audience dissolves.

THE WORK OF
FORGETTING

Anderson's interactive art presents us with a chance to reimagine our relationships with people and things, not by providing us with any idealistic vision of the future but by giving us licence to play for a while in the present. This, in our predominantly consumerist culture, represents a rare opportunity to enact and reinforce social bonds outside the sphere of the market. The Studio itself has more than a purely imaginative function: it provides a model of action, enabling spectators to become participants through the creation of 'social sculpture'. (Here Anderson invokes Joseph Beuys's extended concept of art and his belief in its potential to bring about revolutionary change.) And so we return to the theme of connection, present in Rosenfield's account of our "relating... between moments" in order to create new memories, and in the associations we make with each other in the gallery. Thus, Anderson's work exhorts us to bridge the gap between then and now, while also inviting us to construct a collective identity in the present.

As we participate in Anderson's contemporary ritual, we might consider Walter Benjamin's remarks about the celebrated Penelope, Odysseus's faithful wife. Waiting for his return from the Trojan Wars, Penelope kept her suitors at bay for 20 years by weaving a shroud which she unpicked each evening, claiming she would remarry only when it was finished. Benjamin suggests that in order to keep her husband's memory alive, Penelope must make it the task of each night to forget and the aim of each day to remember. What he calls the "work of forgetting" is poignantly articulated through Anderson's ongoing project. As we struggle and fail to resurrect the past, we may become aware that the stories we tell ourselves are all the truth we need.

Opposite:
Diurnal Drawing, 2011.
In a similar performance to that of Nocturnal Drawings, the Diurnal Drawings are created by turning smaller sheets of paper, held vertically, to create dynamic geometric patterns.

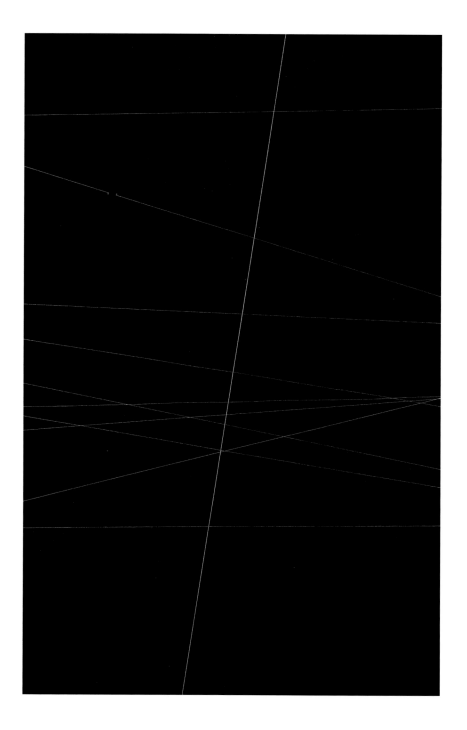

Anderson performing Crystal Time Units at the 55th Venice Biennale, 2013.

THE SCIENCE OF PERCEPTION

–

BY ISRAEL ROSENFIELD

For Alice Anderson, the movements around the object suggest a journey through the memory process: "The weaved objects are not a tribute to the past but a reflection of the present that offers a vision of the changing world."

Alice Anderson's art is a wonderful illustration of the nature and ambiguities of memory. And since memory is central to human and animal psychology and to the functioning of the brain, her work captures a deep aspect of our mental worlds. For animals and humans are constantly moving and this creates a perceptual problem: our sensory worlds are unstable. Our sensory worlds change all the time. What the brain must do – it is probably the principal reason brains evolved – is create a stable, coherent sensory environment that we can understand and use. The brain does this by 'inventing' a range of perceptions, a series of constructs that we 'see', 'hear' and 'feel' when we look, listen and touch. Alice Anderson's objects wound in copper capture an aspect of how the brain makes possible the creation and re-creation of our familiar and unexpected visual worlds by connecting our perceptions over time.

THE MYTH OF STORED
MEMORY IMAGES

A myth has long dominated our conception of memory: that we can accurately remember people, places and things we have seen because images of them have been imprinted and permanently stored in our brains. These images, the myth has it, are the basis of recognition and thought and action. But we are much better at recognition than this would suggest. We recognise people despite changes wrought by ageing. We recognise Picasso's style even in a painting of his that we have never seen before. When we do this, we are doing more than recalling earlier impressions. We are recognising categories that can accommodate variation.

Our capacity to remember, then, is not about recall of a specific image stored somewhere in our brain. Rather it is an ability to organise the world around us into categories – some general, some specific. When we speak of a stored mental image of a friend, which image are we referring to? Unless we understand how we categorise people and things and how we generalise, we will not understand how we remember.

Our conscious recollection – and our thinking and awareness in general – has a continuity over time. Our awareness comes from a flow of perceptions, from the relations among them (both in space and in time), and from our dynamic but constant relation to them that is our unique personal perspective: our subjectivity. An essential part of our subjectivity is the complex network of interconnections that are established by the brain. Hence what appear to be new forms are in fact re-imaginings or re-categorisations of familiar objects. The past becomes the present – as Alice Anderson's art suggests.

This is the significance of Alice Anderson's copper-wound window frames, basketballs and computers. We recognise the window frames, the basketballs and the computers even though they have been transformed. And we see her collaborators moving and winding the objects in copper wire. Here is Anderson's description of her art – a description that parallels what I have written and yet

Opposite:
Articles pinned to the walls
of Anderson's studio.

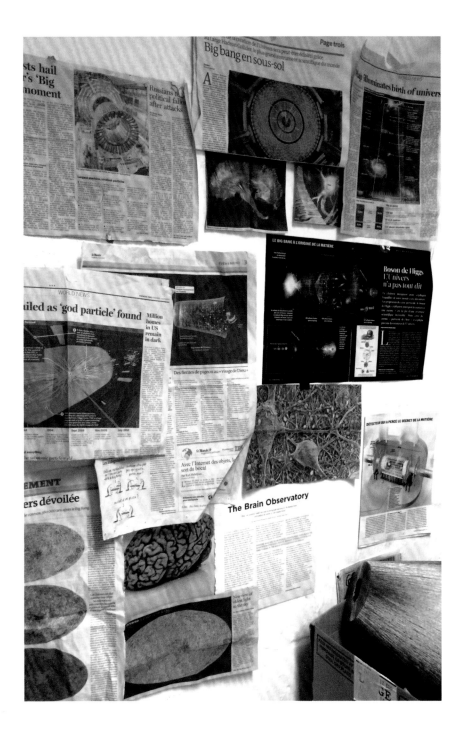

has a somewhat different perspective: "The movements around the object suggest an alternative journey through the memory process. The gestures interrogate how we create, recall, transform and seal the past to imagine the future. To me the 'weaved/mummified' objects are not a tribute to the past but a reflection about the present that gives a vision of the changing world."

Perception, like recognition, is part of a continuity of experience. Our sense of colour, or of smell, or of motion, comes precisely from the flow of perceptions and from the comparisons and categorisations the brain makes from moment to moment. For example, motion pictures give us a sense of continuous movement by means of a series of static images presented in rapid succession. Our conscious experience is not of one static image followed by another. Instead we see motion because our brains create motion, by relating one image to the next. In general, it is this relating, this connecting between moments, not the moments themselves, that is at the heart of our perceptions and recollections. Without this activity of connecting, we would merely perceive a sequence of unrelated stimuli from moment to unrelated moment and we would be unable to transform this experience into knowledge and understanding of the world.

MADAME M'S LOSS OF CONTINUITY

Sometimes this making of connections can fail. Neurological damage can cause a loss of the ability to establish relationships among perceptions and memories, with deeply disturbing consequences.

In 1923 Joseph Capgras and Jean Reboul-Lachaux described a patient, Madame M, who thought her husband and children were impostors. They were, she claimed, very clever look-alikes of the members of her family, and she was not going to let herself be fooled by them. She 'knew' her real husband and children had been kidnapped and the impostors were trying to get her money from her.

Opposite:
Table Tops at Villa Benasconi,
Geneva, 2013.

Capgras and his co-author argued that Madame M's problem came from a disconnection between her emotions and perceptions – she did not have the normal emotional reaction we have upon seeing someone we know intimately. But, more profoundly perhaps, Madame M's neurological breakdown had prevented her recognising the continuity in her family as they even slightly changed over time. As she explained, "You can see it in the details": her husband's moustache was longer than it had been the day before; his hair was combed differently; his skin had become pale and he was wearing a different suit.

In other words, Madame M was confronted by a parade of constantly changing husbands and children – they looked almost alike, but in every case there was something different, something that was misplaced. For her brain, this was the clue that she was dealing with impostors. Her brain was unable to create a synthesis of the constantly changing images she was seeing, unable to connect them, unable to integrate them into a flow of interrelated visualisations of her husband and children. She was getting stuck in the details that change over short periods of time and her memories

Above:
The copper coil in an alarm clock mechanism provided an early inspiration for Anderson.

could no longer accept these changes. She had lost her sense of her husband and children as changeable yet enduring people.

Indeed, Anderson's transformations of familiar objects and people with copper windings can illustrate the abnormality of Capgras syndrome; the failure of recognition of intimate family and friends comes about with the change of merely one detail. But the copper-wound sculptures are transformations on a far larger scale, and we – if we do not have the neurological problem of Madame M – still recognise them.

THE SENSE OF TIME, SELF AND BODY

A grasp of continuity over time is also essential to our own sense of self. While Capgras syndrome involves an inability to relate someone else's present and past, difficulty relating to one's own past can be a feature of autism.

Donna Williams, an autistic writer, has described having problems with "the sense of time and the continuity (or lack of it) in my sense of personal history". To overcome this, she chronicles her life: "Albums with the day's events, key works, objects collected through that day to do with smells and tastes and textures experienced and pictures or photos that capture things that happened that day, can all be put together in a way that can make up month by month accessible libraries. These can be kept year after year so that a person can look through them at any time and get some sort of composite sense of who they are." Anderson's sculptures – while very different from a simple memory album – serve to establish a sense of continuity over time (and space). They connect us not only to the original objects but also to the occasions when they were created and the actions of Anderson and her collaborators.

A similar approach – using details of events to build a sense of time and self – can also help on a smaller scale. One autistic child, when asked questions about what he did "yesterday", "last week" or "a few days ago", simply failed to understand. However, when given a cue, such as

"What did you do at your grandmother's this weekend?", he could answer.

There is a deep relation between our sense of time and our sense of who we are. Equally important – and also a factor in autism – is our sense of our own body.

Tito Mukhnopadhyay, a remarkably insightful autistic boy, described how he struggled with this: "When I was 4 or 5 years old... I hardly realised that I had a body except when I was hungry or when I realised that I was standing under the shower and my body got wet. I needed constant movement, which made me get the feeling of my body. The movement can be of a rotating type or just flapping of my hands. Every movement is proof that I exist. I exist because I can move."

Just as Tito has found movement a way to generate an embodied sense of self, so too is movement an essential element in the creation of Anderson's art, helping her participants to situate themselves and see themselves afresh: "At the studio, when we were all together, the winding repetitive action was similar to collective shamanic dances and people seemed to enjoy it. The bobbins into ceramic jars created rhythms and 'music'. It was like a sort of ceremony, in which the copper colour and wire made people think about themselves and what was around them in a different way."

AWARENESS OF MORE THAN WE SEE

Anderson's copper windings of ordinary objects and her dances with her collaborators show her concern with the creation of coherent perceptions and memories out of apparently chaotic stimuli. She is illustrating how our perceptual worlds are structured from ever-changing stimuli, how they are structured by our pasts, and how they in turn structure our recollections. She is trying to capture the intertwined nature of perception, memory and awareness – namely, that when looking at people and objects we are aware of much more than what we see.

Opposite:
Shelves, 2013.

When facing an acquaintance, we know that we are looking at a three-dimensional person, even if we do not perceive their back at the moment. We know many things about them and their past, and this recollection shapes our perception. It is this awareness that Anderson's copper windings express in their incorporation of the past into the present – the window frame transformed into a wire-wound frame. Her art expresses what consciousness and memory are about: an awareness of something that is not directly perceived.

Consciousness brings more to perception than exists in the present stimulus – it creates something that is not there – and in doing so it helps us make sense of our environment. And so does art. Anderson is exploring the very question that is at the heart of the modern neuroscience – the nature of consciousness – of being aware of something that is not 'really' there.

MOVEMENT
OBJECTS

—

Anderson has developed a technique of weaving that consists of winding copper wire around objects. These performances express Anderson's own belief in art as a powerfully charged communal ritual. Members of the public have been invited to join the 'Studio' and to preserve 'naked' objects by formulating their own methods of weaving the copper thread.

Above: Ford Mustang 1968 in progress, 2015.
Opposite: Crystal Time Units in progress, 2013.

Ropes in progress, 2013–15 (ongoing).

Stairs in progress, 2014.

RECOGNISABLE
OBJECTS

-

This section contains several articles from the artist's studio. Amongst them you will find a pair of spectacles, a basketball and a bicycle, together with a turntable and a Diet Coke bottle. Here are the everyday things that surround us, that will outlive us, and that we often barely acknowledge. Transformed into glowing treasures, they reveal their preciousness and power as symbols of human expression. The flight of stairs ascending into space creates the suspense of an entrance to a sanctuary.

Stairs, 2014.

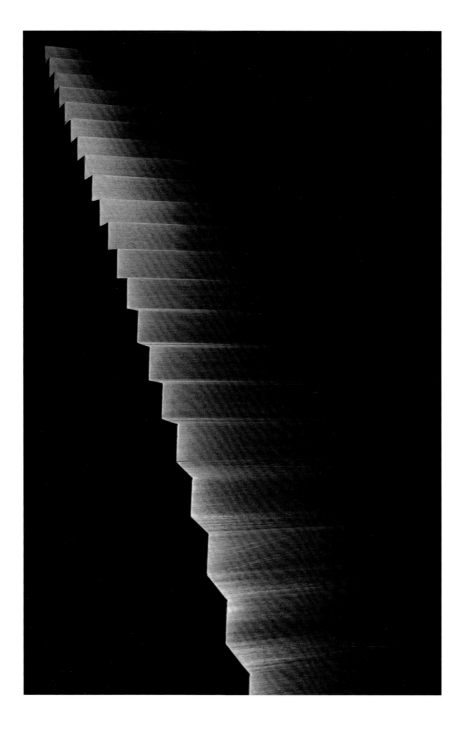

Telescope, 2012.

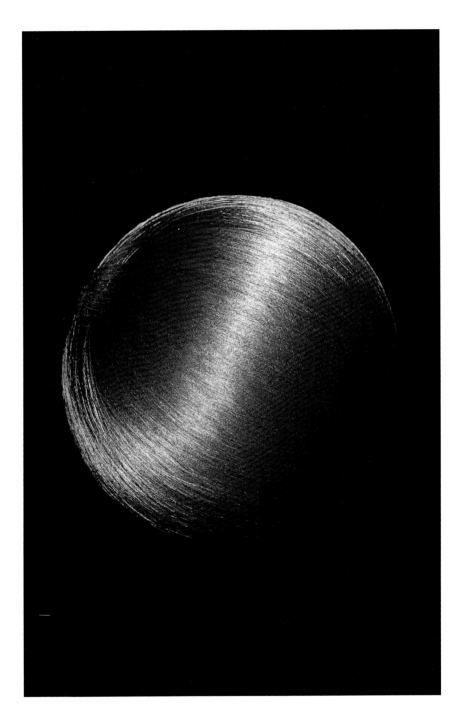

Above: Basketball, 2013.
Opposite: Coke Bottle, 2013.

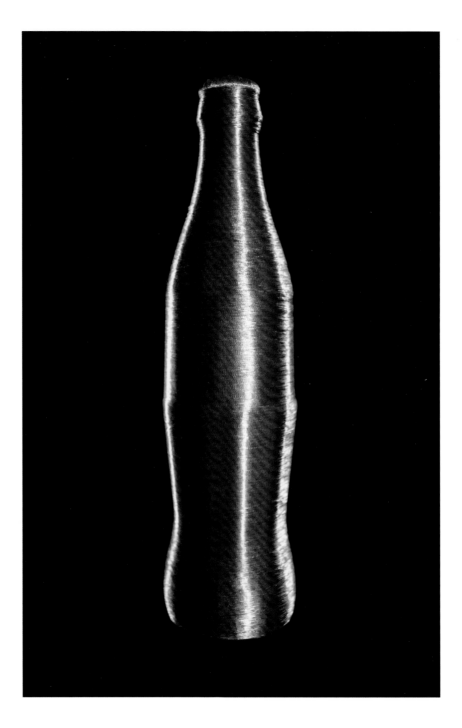

Tagine, 2013.

Above: Turntable, 2012.
Opposite: Bellows, 2014.

Spectacles, 2012.

Above: Bike, 2012–13.
Opposite: Helmet, 2013.

Oil Colours, 2011.

ACCUMULATIONS OF OBJECTS: ASSEMBLAGES

–

In this section strange hybrids are formed from everyday objects. These complex structures take on the appearance of museum pieces or artefacts from other worlds: a tower of repeating symmetrical elements; a composition involving a hoover, a fax machine and two vinyl LPs; table legs stacked vertically like a minimalist icon. Anderson uses the vocabulary of modern abstract sculpture to remind us that history has a way of converting artworks into relics.

Skeletons, Apple Mac Plugs, 2013.

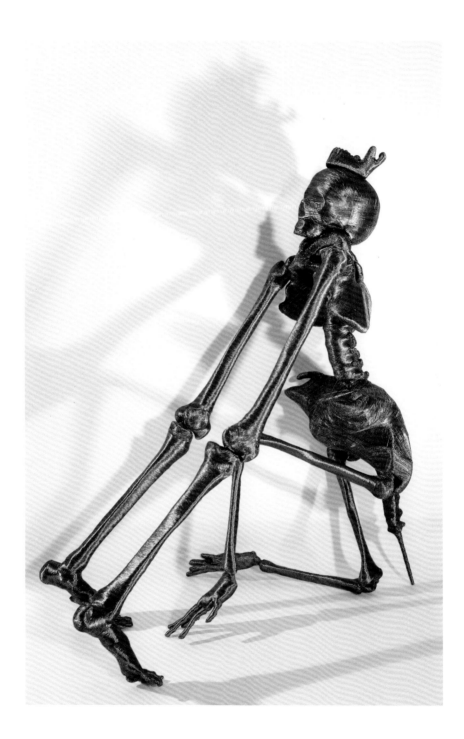

Above: Hoover, Fax Machine, Vinyls, 2013.
Opposite: Wooden Stick, Concorde Plane Toy, Tape Case, CD Case, 2014.

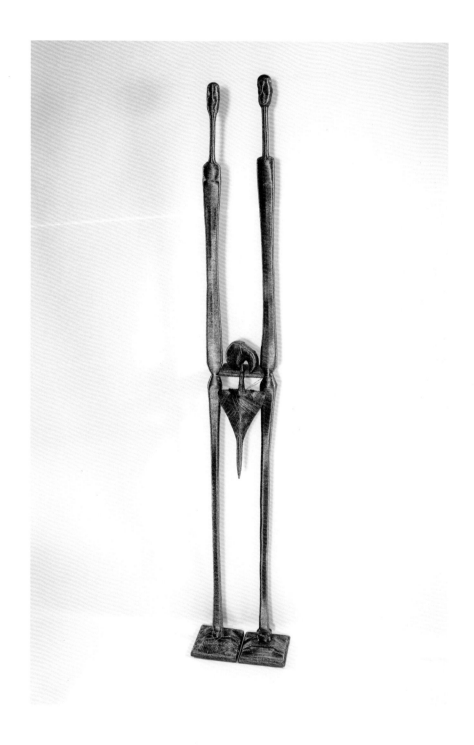

Jars, 2012.

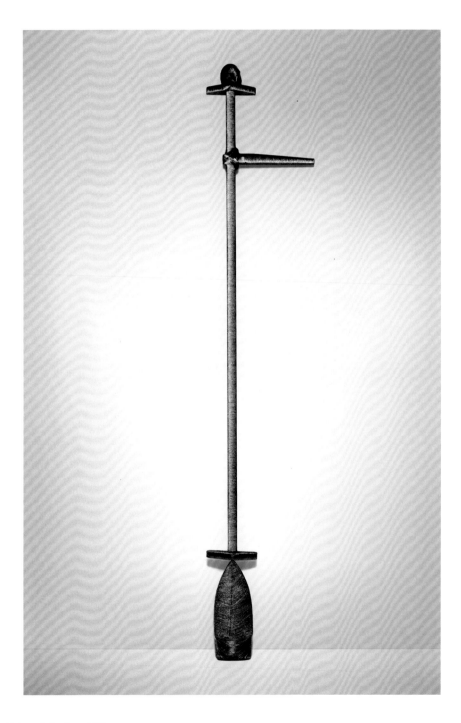

Above: Iron, Fathom, Roller Tape, 2014.
Opposite: Table Legs, 2013.

Ladders, 2014.

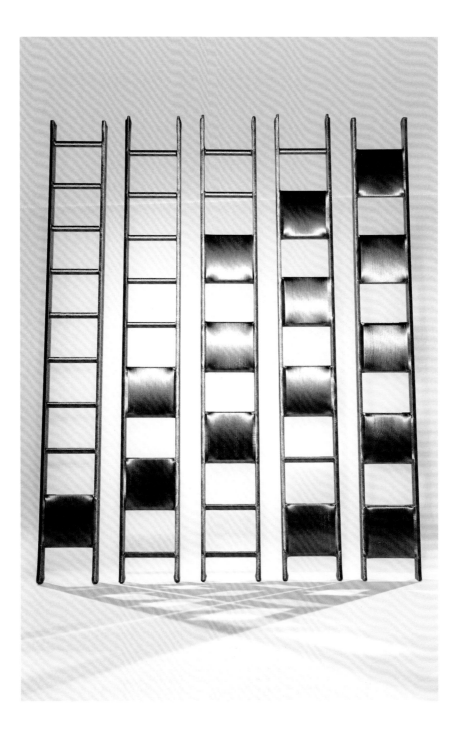

Sketch Books, 2012.

ABSTRACT
OBJECTS

-

These sculptures create a landscape of abstract forms.
Cables of rope ripple through the space, their tangled
arrangements marking out the path. A clock, a VHS player
and a BlackBerry have been simplified to their geometric
principles, highlighting their familiar yet enigmatic natures.
Some table tops from the artist's studio are not yet fully
transformed but on their way to abstraction. Their oblique
surfaces invite us to participate in the act of remembering

Ropes, 2013–15 (ongoing).

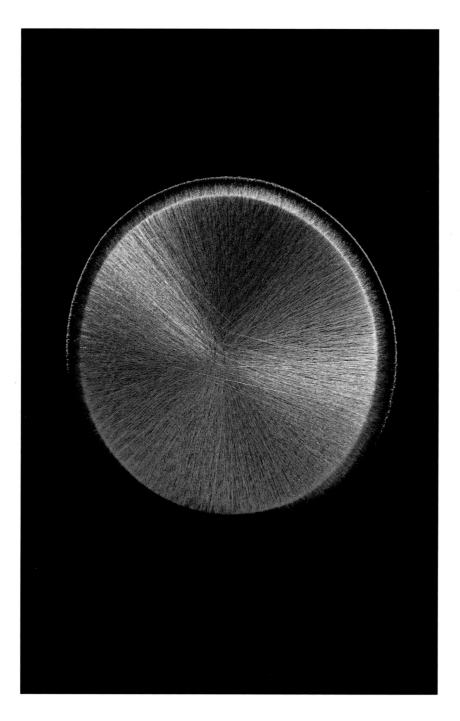

Above: Clock, 2012.
Opposite: VHS Player, 2012.

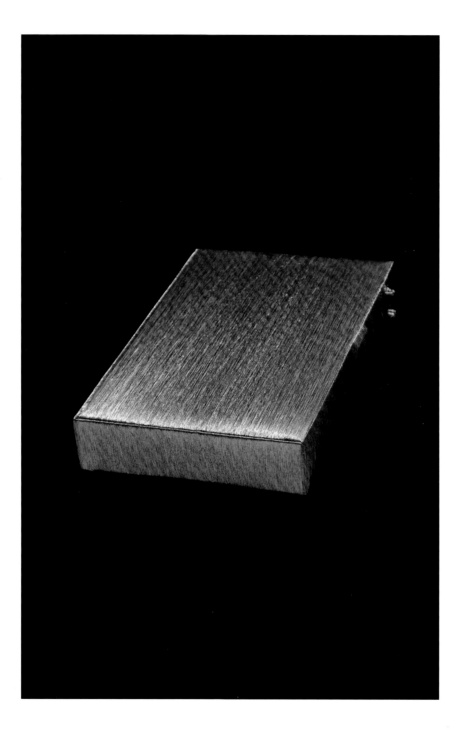

Scale, 2013.

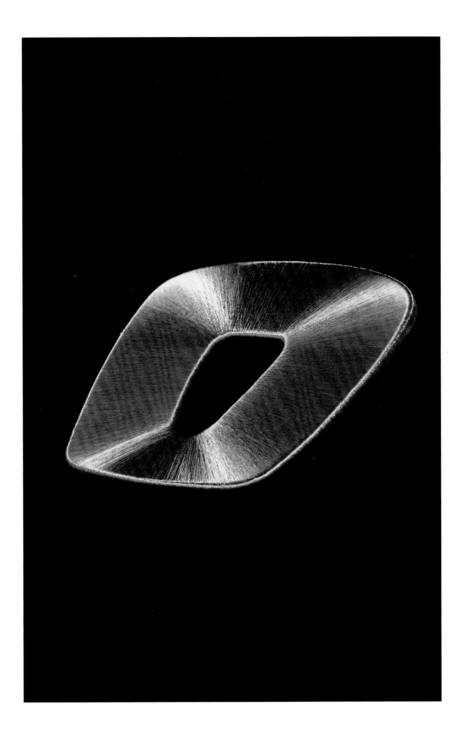

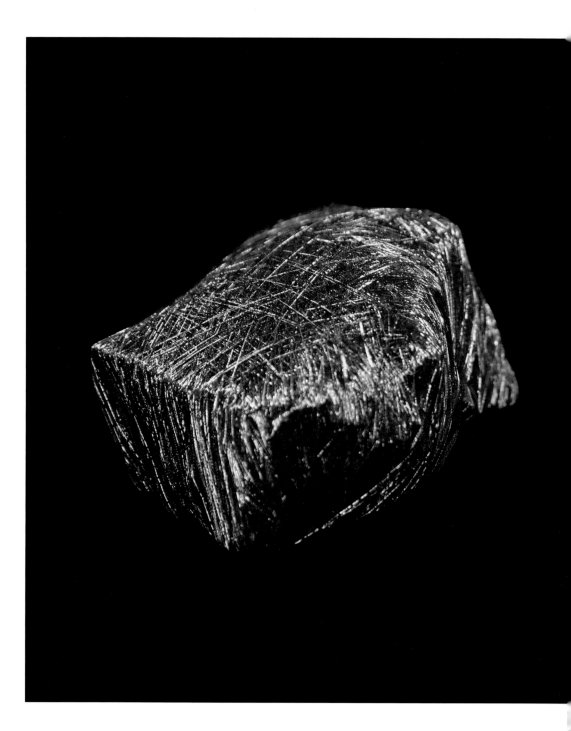

Wall Fragments, 2013.

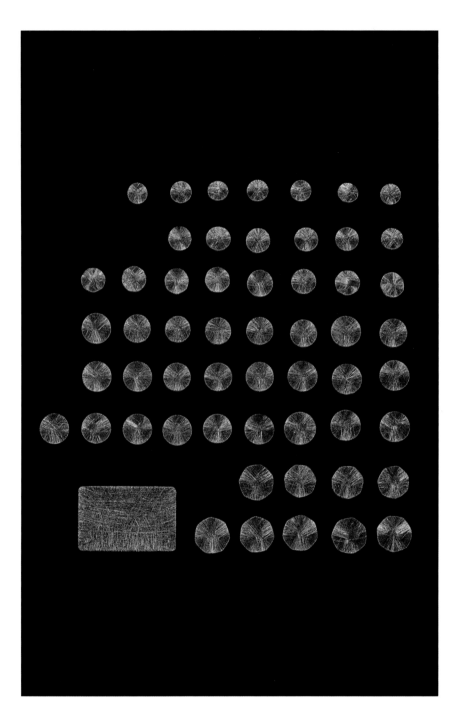

Above: Foreign Coins and Credit Card, 2012.
Opposite: Geometrical Shapes, 2014.

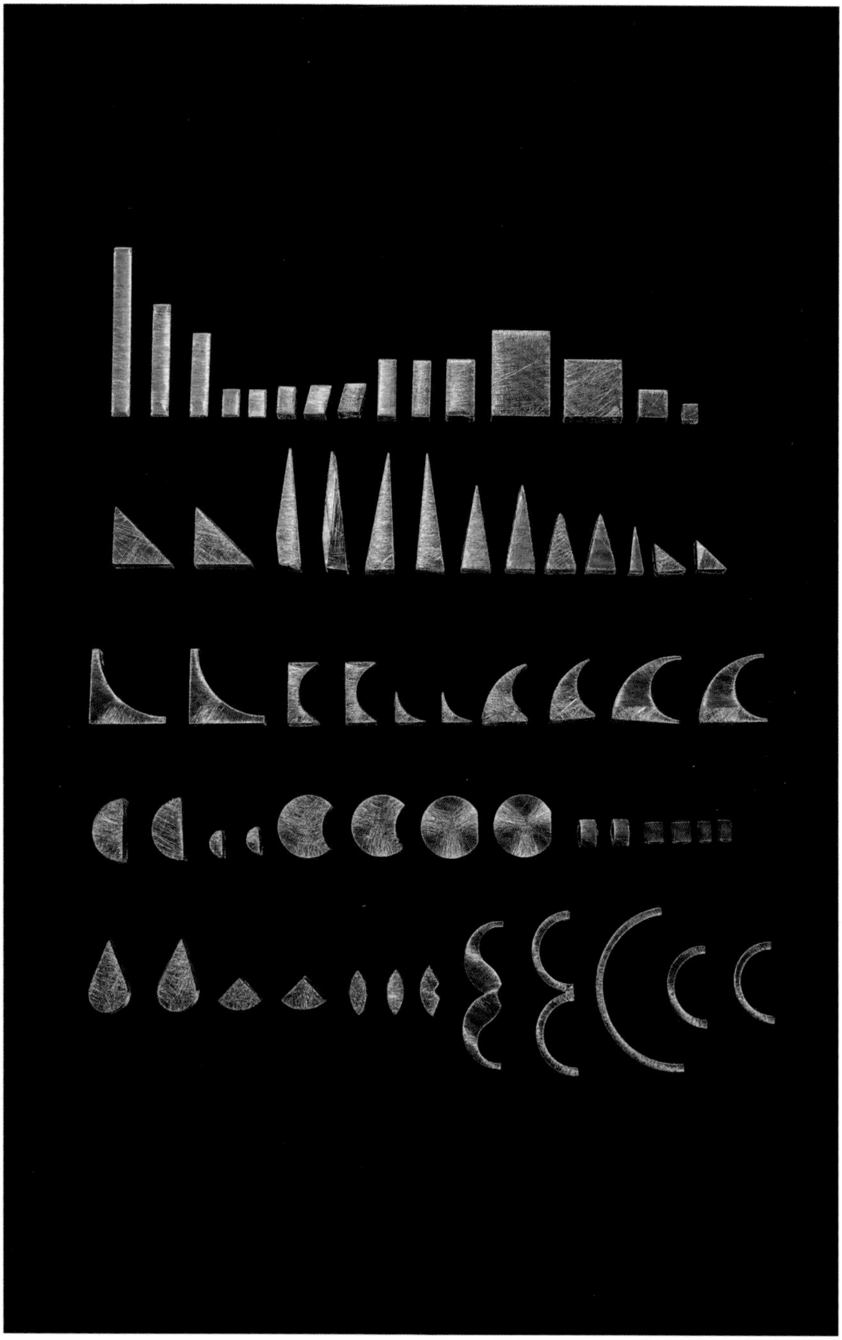

affects everything from the large architectural elements like a door frame and a sash window to the smaller items, a laptop computer and a tea canister. Even the majestic canoe is beginning to twist and to discover its new form. The contours of some objects, such as the satellite dish, render them uncompletable – no matter how many times the bobbin is passed around them they will never be completely covered by the copper wire. Like us, these objects are shaped and altered through the experience of time.

Canoe, 2013.

Wheelbarrow, 2013-14.

Above: Sash Window, 2013.
Opposite: Door Frame, 2013.

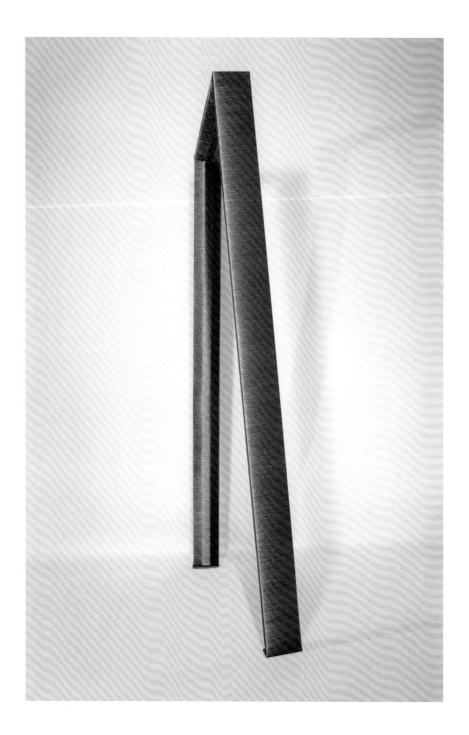

Satellite Dish, 2012–15 (ongoing).

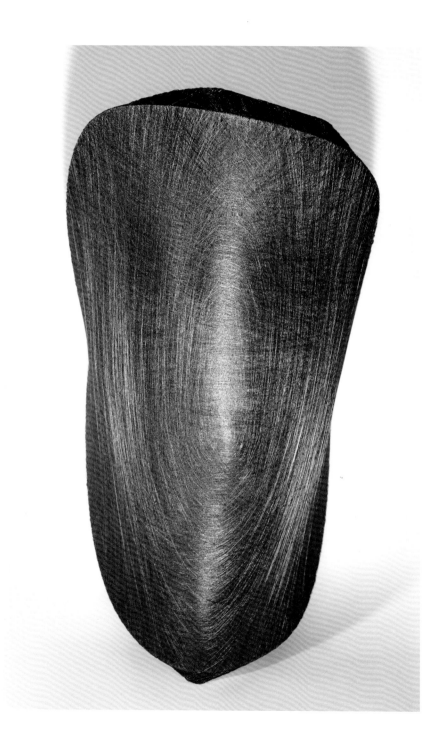

Speakers (with sound), 2014.

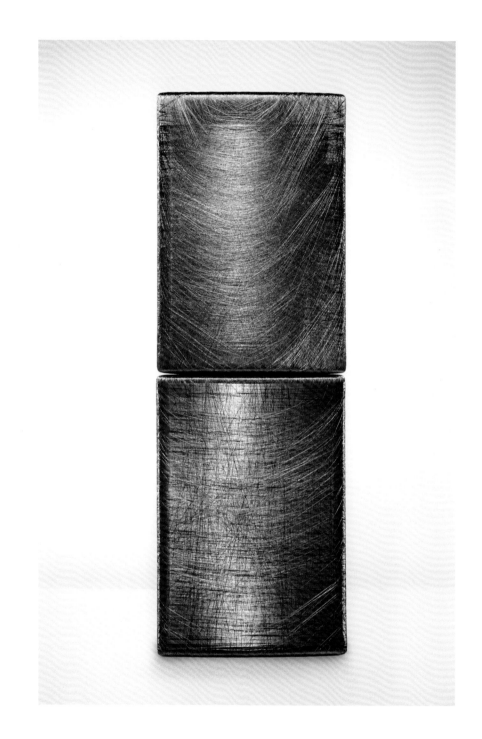

Shelves, 2013.

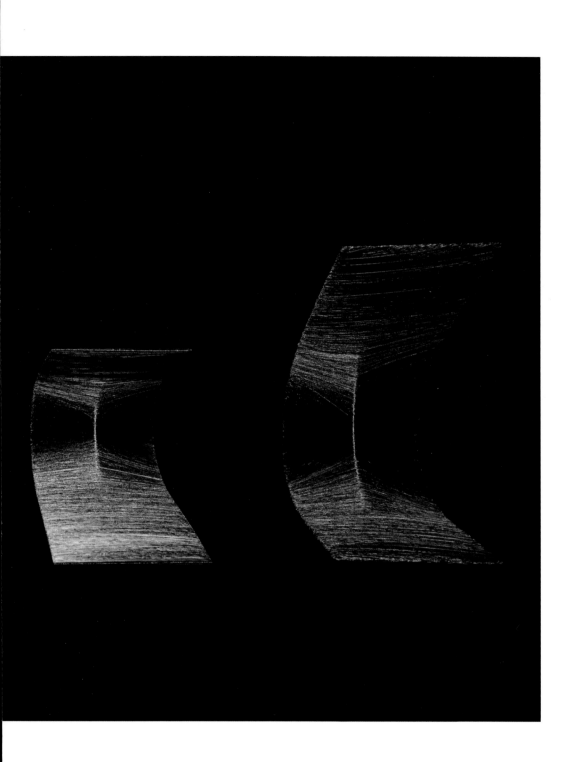

Laptop, 2013.

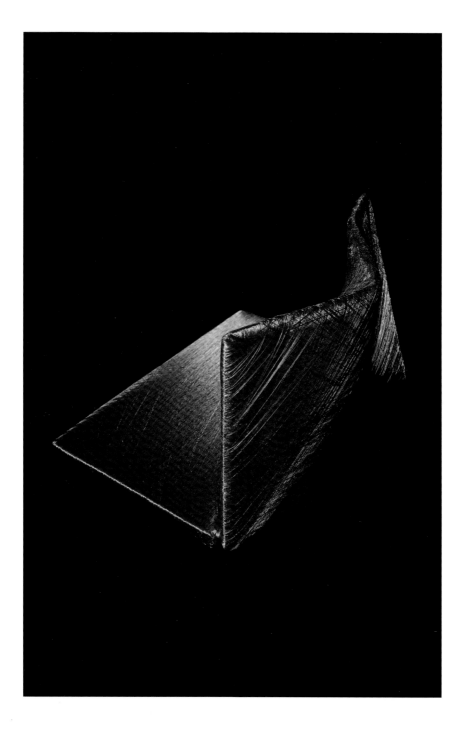

ARTWORK CREDITS

ALICE ANDERSON'S TRAVELLING STUDIO
GEOMETRICAL SHAPES
64 shapes, variable dimensions, copper wire, 2014

SKELETONS, APPLE MAC PLUGS
1 m x 70 cm, copper wire, 2013

NOCTURNAL DRAWINGS
60 cm x 80 cm, paper, copper wire, 2011 (ongoing)

ALICE ANDERSON'S TRAVELLING STUDIO
VINYLS
Variable dimensions, copper wire, 2013
Alice Anderson, Marco Berardi, Kimbal Bumstead,
Jonathan Caruana, Anna Dorofeeva, Ester Escolano,
Anna Fafaliou, Laura Glaser, Jimmy Harris, Sebastian
Hau-Walker, Maciej Piosik, Stella Serpente, Maria Sideri,
Andre Verissimo.

DIURNAL DRAWINGS
20 cm x 30 cm, paper, copper wire, 2011

ALICE ANDERSON'S TRAVELLING STUDIO
CRYSTAL TIME UNITS
70 cm x 5 cm, 30 crystal bars, copper wire, 2013
Alice Anderson, Michele Baron, Katia Beltrame, Laura
Berdusco, Kimbal Bumstead, Jonathan Caruana, Vanessa
Dalozzo, Elena Dolci, Karima El Amrani, Ester Escolano,
Anna Fafaliou, Marta Fassina, Tommaso Franchin, Davide
Gago, Laura Glaser, Sebastian Hau-Walker, Dragos Licar,
Margherita Lotti, Diane Malet, Leanna Moran, Monica
Pastore, Maria Vittoria Piana, Anna Maria Pinaka,
Alexander Ramsden, Fabrizio Rigutti, Stella Serpente,
Alice Tatge, Benedetta Vialli, Francesca Zuccarello.

ALICE ANDERSON'S TRAVELLING STUDIO
TABLE TOPS
2.44 m x 1.22 m, copper wire, 2013 (ongoing)
Alice Anderson, Katia Beltrame, Marco Berardi, Kimbal
Bumstead, Jonathan Caruana, Ester Escolano, Anna
Fafaliou, Laura Glaser, Sebastian Hau-Walker, Josue
Lozano, Diane Malet, Leanna Moran, Lucile Moulin, Janina
Rajakangas, Alexander Ramsden, Stella Serpente, Maria
Sideri, Alice Tatge, Andre Verissimo.

SHELVES
1 m x 15 cm, copper wire, 2013

FORD MUSTANG 1968
4.56 m x 1.78 m, copper wire, 2015 (in progress)

ALICE ANDERSON'S TRAVELLING STUDIO
ROPES
250 m of paper ropes, copper wire, 2013-15 (ongoing)
Alice Anderson, Chalie Chalosri, Alfonso Costilla Gamaza,
Marta De Frutos, Anna Fafaliou, Virginie Herbert,
Dionysia Kypraiou, Josue Lozano, Christina Makri, Daniela
Piedrahita, Laurin von der Osten-Sacken, Sophie Wiltshire.

ALICE ANDERSON'S TRAVELLING STUDIO
STAIRS
7 m x 80 cm x 4 m, copper wire, 2014
Alice Anderson, Marta De Frutos, Anna Fafaliou, Virginie
Herbert, Josue Lozano, Christina Makri, Daniela Piedrahita,
Laurin von der Osten-Sacken, Sophie Wiltshire.

TELESCOPE
1.50 m x 80 cm, copper wire, 2012

BASKETBALL
50 cm, copper wire, 2013

COKE BOTTLE
20.5 cm x 6 cm, copper wire, 2013

TAGINE
18 cm x 25 cm diameter, copper wire, 2013

TURNTABLE
15 cm x 28 cm, copper wire, 2012

BELLOWS
3.5 cm x 10 cm, copper wire, 2014

SPECTACLES
14 cm x 11 cm, copper wire, 2012

BIKE
1.68 cm x 60 cm, copper wire, 2012-13

HELMET
15 cm x 20 cm, copper wire, 2013

OIL COLOURS
Variable dimensions, copper wire, 2011

HOOVER, FAX MACHINE, VINYLS
1.40 m x 28 cm, copper wire, 2013

WOODEN STICK, CONCORDE PLANE TOY,
TAPE CASE, CD CASE
1.60 m x 4 cm, copper wire, 2014

JARS
4 m x 27 cm, copper wire, 2012

IRON, FATHOM, ROLLER TAPE
1.52 m x 10 cm, copper wire, 2014

TABLE LEGS
1.4 m x 40 cm, copper wire, 2013

LADDERS
3 m x 30 cm, copper wire, 2014

ALICE ANDERSON'S TRAVELLING STUDIO
SKETCH BOOKS
30 sketch books, variable dimensions, copper wire, 2012
Alice Anderson, Katia Beltrame, Sabina Borelli, Kimbal
Bumstead, Sofie Burgoyne, Ester Escolano, Anna Fafaliou,
Laura Glaser, Sebastian Hau-Walker, Sebastian Kim, Josue
Lozano, Diane Malet, Maxime Marboeuf, Leanna Moran,
Lucile Moulin, Daniela Piedrahita, Alexander Ramsden,
Stella Serpente, Carys Staton, Lee Sullivan.

CLOCK
1.5 m x 30 cm, copper wire, 2012

VHS PLAYER
40 cm x 26 cm, copper wire, 2012

SCALE
32 cm x 32 cm, copper wire, 2013

WALL FRAGMENTS
Variable dimensions, copper wire, 2013

ALICE ANDERSON'S TRAVELLING STUDIO
FOREIGN COINS & CREDIT CARD
Variable dimensions, copper wire, 2012
Alice Anderson, Chalie Chalosri, Alfonso Costilla Gamaza,
Marta De Frutos, Anna Fafaliou, Virginie Herbert, Josue
Lozano, Christina Makri, Daniela Piedrahita, Laurin von der
Osten-Sacken, Sophie Wiltshire.

ALICE ANDERSON'S TRAVELLING STUDIO
CANOE
5.50 m x 90 cm x 60 cm, copper wire, 2013
Alice Anderson, Marie Armbruster, Zoe Authier, Damien
Berger, Faustine Berger, Jocelyne Berger, Françoise
Berney, Roland Berney, Dominique Bonnel, Yolande
Chaleil, Nathalie Chatelain, Dany Chauvin, Lauriane
Chevallier, Annaick Choquet, Gaelle Choquet, Laurette
Conio, Violaine Dautremont, Remy Doucet, Jacky
Desarmenien, Christiane Fayolle, Eva Ferlat, Corinne
Gambi, Yvette Gauthier, Apolline Gerbet, Marie Gerbet,
Gilles Girod, Anne Gresard, Françoise Guerin, Yves
Guerin, Cathy Herault, Marcela Iriarte, Brigitte Joncourt,
Bernadette Lacroix, Françoise Lechenault, Ben Magrin,
Isabelle Magrin, Claude Mignon, Genevieve Nicod,
Alice Parrod, Clara Pellegrini, Didier Pellegrini, Therese
Petithuguenin, Christophe Podico, Irene Poix-Daude,
Brigitte Renaud, Clarisse Renaud, Joseph Renaud,
Madeleine Renaud, Valerie Renaud, Edith Rigoulot, Sophie
Robbe, Catherine Sauvonnet, Monique Viennet.

WHEELBARROW
60 cm x 56 cm x 70 cm, copper wire, 2013-14

SASH WINDOW
120 cm x 90 cm, copper wire, 2013

DOOR FRAME
200 cm x 80 cm, copper wire, 2013

SATELLITE DISH
1 m x 50 cm, copper wire, 2012-15 (ongoing)

SPEAKERS (WITH SOUND)
1.60 m x 20 cm, copper wire, 2014

LAPTOP
27 cm x 35 cm, copper wire, 2013

Further Reading

Walter Benjamin, 'The Image of Proust' (1929). In *Illuminations: Essays and Reflections*, ed. Hannah Arendt (Schocken, 1968).

Marcel Duchamp, *The Creative Act* (Schocken, 1969).

Maurice Merleau-Ponty, *The Phenomenology of Perception* (Routledge, 1962).

James Putnam, 'Alice Anderson: From Dance To Sculpture' (Espoo Museum of Modern Art, 2012).

Oliver Sacks, 'Speak, Memory' (*New York Review of Books*, 21 February 2013).

–

Acknowledgements

The authors and editors would like to thank all the staff and supporters who helped to make this book and exhibition possible, especially: Alice Anderson, Marcela Iriarte, Maud Jacquin, Malcolm Chivers, Zoe Middleton, Luke Currall, Melanie Stacey, Natalie Coe, Georgia Monk, and Janice Forde.

Alice Anderson is very grateful to Kate Forde, James Peto and Ken Arnold, who believed in *Memory Movement Memory Objects* and supported it from scratch.